How to
an Autis
Christmas

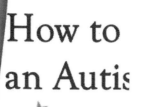

Autistic
Christmas

*Every child
is a gift xxx*

Written by Autistic Author

Emma Kendall

First published in 2019
by M and R Publishing
PO Box 2016
Andover
SP10 9JQ

contact@mandrpublishing.co.uk

Copyright © Emma Kendall 2019
Printed digitally since 2019

www.emma-kendall.co.uk

Cover by M and R Publishing
Title font by Sam Wang (1001 Free Fonts)

ISBN 978-1-70127-221-7

AUTISTIC CHRISTMAS

Contents

Contents

Contents

Acknowledgements

I would like to say a huge thank you to all the families of autistic children, and individuals that have shared their experiences with me. Without you, I wouldn't have been able to learn and cover as many topics as I have.

My warmest appreciation must go to all the people that have supported my son and me on our autism journey.

The people I truly appreciate are Lesley and Sian, my son's pre-school and school teachers, Chris - my university tutor, and my immediate family members.

My heartfelt thanks go to Simon and Nic. We've shared so many wonderful Christmases together, making the most amazing memories. We miss you so much!

A very special thank you must go to my in-laws Stephen and Susan. Fifteen years ago, you took me on as your own and have always treated me like a daughter. I can't put into words how grateful I am for all of your support.

I also want to say a huge thanks to my parents and step-parents for providing me and my children with many happy Christmas memories. You always make it extra special for my children and I truly appreciate you all.

Last but not least, my biggest thanks go to my husband and my children. I count my blessings every day for the love and happiness that you bring into my life.

About the Author

Emma Kendall specialises in supporting adults, children and parents of children that are diagnosed with an autism spectrum disorder (ASD).

Emma is the author of Perfectly Autistic: An ASD Post Diagnosis Support Book for Parents. The book has been a huge hit within the autism community. Receiving excellent feedback and reaching the bestsellers lists on Amazon.

Emma was diagnosed with Asperger's syndrome/high functioning autism in her early thirties. She also has many family members diagnosed with an autism spectrum disorder, including her son.

Emma has completed academic studies with the University of Birmingham (UK), specialising in Autism: Special Education (BPhil), where she graduated with a first-class degree.

Her educational background includes qualifications in Counselling, Communication, and Personal Skills.

To join my FaceBook Page:

Search for 'Emma Kendall Author'

To receive updates on future releases, bonus content and more, visit:

www.emma-kendall.co.uk

Introduction

Christmas is known as the most wonderful time of the year. It's full of celebrations, parties, festive decorations, shopping, eating, sharing gifts and spending time with loved ones.

For parents of autistic children, Christmas can also be the most stressful time of the year. The festive season can bring lots of excitement and joy for children, but equally, Christmas can also bring disruption to routine, sleeping and eating habits, and so on as well as creating additional anxieties, social exhaustion and changes in behaviour.

Christmas can be a socially demanding time of the year, both within the family unit and at preschool or school, which means one thing for your child: lots of *communicating and interacting*.

Communication differences in those on the autism spectrum is a typical characteristic which is known to create additional issues. Those differences can impact how an autistic child interacts, processes information, reciprocates language and converses with others.

The social demands associated with Christmas can bring many challenges. Therefore, it is important to recognise how to support your child to help reduce difficulties.

There are also lots of sensory aspects associated with Christmas such as:

Sight   -   Decorations, lights, costumes, displays.
Sound   -   Parties, Christmas music, new toys.
Touch   -   Opening gifts, new clothes, decorations.
Taste   -   New foods, changes in meals, overeating.
Smells   -   Candles, perfumes, foods/drinks, log fires.

Sensory difficulties are another characteristic associated with autism spectrum disorders. This is another important aspect that needs to be recognised and understood when supporting an autistic child.

Santa (Father Christmas) can also be very confusing for autistic children;

Does his sleigh really fly?

Do his elves really watch you and relay information back to the North Pole?

Why does Santa only come once a year with a sack full of toys?

For some autistic children, the whole make-believe aspect of Christmas can be a challenge in itself.

First, there's the Christmas wish list and what to put on it, the receiving and opening of presents, how to reciprocate, communicate, react and respond. The

Christmas wish list and receiving of gifts are what Christmas is all about when you have children, but when you have an autistic child, it is surprising how many anxieties can erupt from something which to others seems so simple.

Christmas can also be a very unpredictable time of year for autistic children. For parents, Christmas is a little more foreseeable. You may already have set traditions that you inherited from your parents and have continued since childhood. Such as places you may visit, types of food you eat, games you play, Christmas movies you watch, and so on.

We know Christmas comes at the same time every year, therefore planning and preparations for autistic children can be a good idea to prevent additional stress. We can support them by providing basic routines, coping strategies, comfort and predictability.

Being autistic, a parent to an autistic son and someone who has supported many families of autistic children over the years, I have learnt that Christmas is one of the most unpredictable, unsettling, and stressful times of the year. These experiences have taught me that there are many families who require support and want to gain a deeper understanding of the complexities associated with autism and Christmas, prompting me to write this book.

This book will cover a range of topics to help you understand the complexities and diverse characteristics associated with autism throughout the festive season, including:

Delays in development, language ability/disability, sensory differences/difficulties, learning difficulties, behavioural differences, and so on.

The chapters will cover the following:

> The complex misunderstandings and literal thinking associated with Christmas traditions.
>
> How Christmas impacts sensory perception, including associated triggers and stressors.
>
> Adapting to Christmas routines and changes in your child's environment.
>
> The social aspects associated with Christmas, and how to prepare your child when going to family or social events.
>
> How to support your child in an educational setting.
>
> Challenges associated with Christmas presents.
>
> Choosing the perfect gift.
>
> Christmas planning and preparations, and much more.

I typically focus on preschool and school-aged children. I cover a range of topics which cover different aspects of abilities and limitations. Because of the complex nature of autism spectrum disorders, you may find some topics to be useful, and some not. This is because I personally haven't met your child, so it's very difficult to provide information specific to a child without knowing their personal differences and difficulties.

I will use the term autistic or autism as collective terms when referring to people diagnosed with autism or an associated autism spectrum disorder.

I will also use the term disorder, as opposed to condition because it is the universally recognised term and used in current literature and legislation.

I hope you enjoy the book, and most of all, I hope I can help you with some new ideas on how to support your child over the festive season.

Chapter 1

Christmas Misunderstandings and Literal Thinking

The Christmas season is a special time of the year. We see big decorated trees being brought into homes and families welcoming the idea of a cheerful guy in a big red suit popping down their chimney, delivering heart-warming gifts to put under the tree. He is helped by his little army of elves that work tirelessly to make sure every child gets that special Christmas wish.

As adults, we know Christmas is full of fun and fairy tales, but to children on the autism spectrum, all these festive traditions can be overwhelming, confusing and often generate unwanted anxieties.

A child may question:

> "What is Christmas? Why do we have Christmas? What are we celebrating? Why are gifts being exchanged? Why are there so many traditions? Why

do we have a decorated tree in the house?"

There are countless questions that can provoke many answers.

It is well known that no two autistic people are exactly the same. Therefore, each and every child will experience Christmas differently compared to the next.

These differences can be because of:

Language ability/disability:

> Their level of language comprehension. Is your child verbal, preverbal or non-verbal? How does your child use communication and social skills to interact?

Sensory processing:

> Does your child have distinct responses to specific lights, smells, tastes, textures and noises?

Understanding of their environment:

> Does your child have delays in development? Do they have an advanced imagination or an overactive mind? Do they experience difficulty adapting to changes, new routines, people, or places?

Differing levels of emotional stress:

> Does your child have anxieties? Can they regulate their emotions, anger and stress? Are they easily

triggered? Does your child experience autistic meltdowns and/or withdrawal behaviours?

Limited flexibility of thought:

Does your child view and understand things literally? Or have a limited imagination or inability to use pretend play, and struggle to see things from a different perspective (have own ideas of how things should be)?

Need for repetition and predictability:

Does your child prefer to play with the same toys, wear the same/similar clothes, eat specific foods, etc.? Do they require structured daily routines and prompting with what is happening next?

All these autistic intricacies impact how a child relates and responds to Christmas.

Common Confusing Aspects of Christmas

If your child mostly views Christmas in literal terms, there may be several confusing aspects that can be difficult for them to comprehend (especially in their younger years) such as:

Who is Santa?
Why does he have lots of different names such as Santa Claus, Father Christmas, Saint Nicholas or

Père Noël?

Why does the Santa at the supermarket look different from the one I see on TV?

How can he be in so many places at the same time?

Where does Santa come from?

How does Santa get down the chimney and what happens if there is no chimney?

Why doesn't he just use the front door?

Why do we bring a tree into the house?

What are the decorations for?

Why do we eat mince pies, Christmas dinner and Christmas pudding?

Why won't Santa bring me a real unicorn, or send me on a real spaceship ride?

Is the Elf on the shelf really watching everything?

Does the naughty or nice list really exist?

It is your child's understanding and thought process that will no doubt impact the way you explain to him/her who Santa is and why we have these Christmas traditions.

This is when we have to be mindful of what we are saying. It is common for autistic children to become angry when they find out that Santa is a fictional character and that it has been you and your family who have provided the presents for them over the years.

Typically for autistic children the issue isn't with Santa not being real, but more so the fact that they have been lied to.

Avoiding the truth can cause anger and resentment because the people they put their trust in have been deceitful not just about Santa and the gifts, but also about other things like being on the naughty or nice list. Let's be honest, it's not uncommon to hear of parents bribing their children with "If you don't behave, Santa will know and he won't come."

If you are making a bold statement, you will need to recognise what additional effect it may have on the child's behaviour. Will it trigger them? Or do they respond well to bold direct statements?

Christmas is very much about spreading joy and bringing families together. Parenting can be extra special because you get to see the magic of Christmas through your child's eyes. It's a cherished time where bonds can develop deeper, and we can form happy memories. But if your child has difficulties in dealing with the Christmas period, it can make parenting a lot more challenging.

Literal Thinking

A huge aspect of Christmas is the fictional make-believe tales that we typically expect children to believe.

In the past twenty years, we have seen a dramatic change in technology and children's toys. There are apps and websites that allow you to put in your location and follow Santa around the world, counting down the minutes until he is due to land at your address.

There are websites that can produce personalised video

messages from Santa and his elves. Just by simply uploading photos and providing personalised information, they can customise the message for your child.

We also have surveillance toys such as the Elf on the Shelf, dummy CCTV Cameras (e.g. Santa Cam), mini fake elf/fairy doors that stick on the skirting board to let them in and out, baubles for the tree that are specifically made to look like CCTV camera's, and much more.

One of the more traditional make-believe aspects of Christmas that we have seen for many years is taking your child to visit Santa in his Grotto. We see more and more shops and companies offering the service for parents to bring their children so they can sit with Santa, have their photo taken and receive a gift.

These aspects are all put in place to provide fun and enjoyment and keep the magic of Christmas alive and some parents also use them to reinforce good behaviour. But if your child has difficulty understanding or using their imagination, or if they have an overactive mind, then it will no doubt cause them to present differences in behaviour.

Will your child become anxious knowing that Santa (a stranger) is coming into their house at night on Christmas Eve? Some children will find the whole concept to be petrifying. If you have taught your child to not talk to strangers or to not let them in your home, this may impact how they feel about the situation. So, it's important to recognise if your child needs the Santa coming into the house situation explaining to them or not, so you can recognise if you are creating additional anxieties.

If you use the Elf on the Shelf, will it make your child worry about little people being in the house? Do they already have night terrors, fear of monsters or are uneasy with sleeping on their own?

If you implement a *naughty* Elf on the Shelf that likes to get up to mischief whilst everyone is sleeping, is it going to teach your child it is funny to be naughty? Will they copy? Or will they distinguish the differences in the fun aspect?

If your child is an over thinker and has underlying anxieties with unpredictability and change, as parents, you have to be mindful that some of these make-believe factors could produce additional behaviours. Ask yourself, is your child trying to make sense of things, or struggling to understand the situation?

If you are implementing these traditions, it is important to observe your child's reactions and responses to gauge their level of comprehension and how it impacts them.

We can view another aspect of literal thinking from a factual stance. There are many children on the autism spectrum that enjoy learning specific facts, especially when referring to history. For example, why do people do certain things, how do things work, what are the rules? I have come across older children saying things such as,

"It took Phileas Fogg eighty days to travel around

the world, it's impossible for Santa to visit every house in one night."

"If Santa was real, he would visit poor people and bring them food hampers. He wouldn't let them starve at Christmas time."

"Christmas trees are historically Pagan and so are Christian traditions, I'm neither, so why do we have a tree in our house?"

Again, this is another time when we have to be mindful of how your child retains and processes information.

There are many autistic children that are completely opposite when understanding Christmas and everything it brings. Some children will be totally oblivious to all the changes. Therefore, the festive season doesn't impact them in the slightest. This generally applies in particular to children with developmental delays, intellectual disabilities or specific learning difficulties.

We could view this as a positive, because the festive changes don't necessarily impact them. But for some parents, it can be quite upsetting when a child doesn't understand. Not because they are angry or annoyed that their child is autistic, but because they want their child to join in and enjoy the magic and celebrations.

Personal Experiences

My son didn't understand the concept of Christmas and presents until he was around five years old, he was both developmentally delayed and pre-verbal. Even though I would attempt to make Christmas extra special by decorating the house, playing Christmas music, wearing Christmas-themed clothes, etc., he was still completely oblivious to everything going on around him. Christmas Day was just another day; he had no interest in opening gifts because he didn't understand the concept of Santa and gift-giving.

As a parent, it goes against everything you imagine Christmas with children to be like. So, adjusting to how your child views Christmas can be quite overwhelming and complex at times. It takes time and effort to understand how your child processes the festive season, and what adaptations you need to put in place.

My son was two years old when we first took him to visit Santa at his Grotto. I wasn't too sure how he would respond or react. As soon as we went in, my son started crying and screaming, which turned into a full-on autistic meltdown. Back then, my son had difficulty with new faces and people. We had tried to prepare him by showing him lots of pictures and images on TV, but taking him to see the real thing was just too much for him to tolerate. I learned very quickly to not put my son in a situation like that again. My son gained nothing from the experience, and neither did we as parents.

Now that my son is older and has gained full speech, I can ask him what he is comfortable with. At the age of eight, my son still can't tolerate visiting Santa, the thought of it provokes anxieties surrounding the social aspects of being one to one with a stranger, so I don't force him, and just simply accept that there are some traditions that he doesn't need to take part in or follow.

As a child, I wasn't developmentally or verbally delayed; I was opposite to my son. I remember having an extremely vivid imagination and retained information very well. When I look back and think of the Christmas tales that my parents introduced, I have a strong memory of my dad *jokingly* telling me and my siblings that there was a fly on the wall watching everything, and if we were misbehaved Santa would find out. It turned out a few years down the line that what I thought was a fly on the wall, was, in fact, a nail in the wall.

Yet, I have this very clear memory of really believing everything my parents told me. With that, I believed the whole concept of Santa and his elves, so when I finally came to realise it was all a fairy tale, I was quite disheartened. But what I love, even at almost forty years old, is that I still have these magical imaginative memories of Christmas as a child.

Key Points

- Remember to be mindful of your child's understanding of Christmas traditions and fairy tales.
- Recognise that your child may need things explaining to them in an honest and simple to understand manner.

Chapter 2

How Christmas can Impact Sensory Perception

Christmas time can introduce a whole new range of sensory triggers that can impact an autistic child and how they respond to their environment. Sensory perception is an important characteristic that needs to be identified and acknowledged by parents when supporting and tending to their child's specific needs.

Being aware of your child's sensory difficulties will not only give you a better understanding of your child's behaviours and triggers, but also enable you to help them understand why and how they react and respond to the world through their senses.

Sensory aspects that can impact a child are:

Sight

Over-stimulation from lights flashing or flickering too bright or too dark or rooms filled with fluorescent lighting can strain the eyes.

If your child is triggered by certain lights, give them sunglasses or glasses with coloured/tinted lenses, a baseball cap or hooded top that they can fold over their face to shield their eyes.

If you have a younger child that can be carried or placed in a pram, take a lightweight blanket or a cover with you when outside of the house so you can shelter them from harsh unpredictable lights.

Teach your child to put their hands over their eyes when the light is too sensitive for them, so you can recognise that they are uncomfortable, enabling you to rectify the situation.

A child may experience visual over-stimulation caused by too much screen time i.e., television, computer games and electronic tablets. It's important to recognise if this is a visual trigger which impacts behaviour or sleep patterns.

They may become triggered when over-stimulated in their environment, both at home or when visiting places, for example, when they are in unfamiliar busy, crowded or cluttered spaces. If there are lots of children running around, screaming and shouting, coming into their comfort zone or personal space, this may also trigger certain children.

Spending too much time looking at Christmas/shop displays can become visually overwhelming.

Smell

Sensitivity to certain fragrances such as perfumes, fabric conditioners, candles, food/drinks, burning logs, flowers, etc.

If smells are too strong, give your child a trigger word to use to inform you when they are experiencing difficulties.

You could keep a handkerchief in your coat pocket (or give one to your child) when out of the house, so you can put it over their nose to block the distressing smells if need be.

Taste

Sensitivity to food tastes, for example, too spicy, bland, bitter or sweet.

Food textures can feel too soft, hard, bitty, chewy or crunchy.

The child could be over/under-stimulated by food, for example, eating too much too often, or too little.

Have an aversion to certain foods, e.g., they will only eat specific food groups.

Need structure regarding meals, for example, putting the food in a specific order on the plate, not touching, no sauces or added flavourings.

If your child has food sensitivities, eating out can become problematic. When eating in restaurants or with family and friends, try to keep their meal simple. Do not introduce too many new foods if you know this will trigger them. Or, pack up a container with foods to take with you (or if possible, take a meal that you can reheat), so at least you know your child will eat something familiar to them.

If you are holding a dinner party, let your child see, smell and taste the foods before your guests arrive, so there are no anxieties or uncertainties when sitting down for your meal.

You could go one step further and take the stress out of eating by letting your child eat before everyone else or let them sit on their own. You could always put a plate of food aside for them to eat after the guests have left. Either way, if your child has food sensitivities, taking the stress out of it will make the process of eating much easier both for you and your child.

Touch

Sensitivity to certain fabrics, clothes, labels in clothes and textures.

Need to be comforted by weighted blankets, being rocked, hugged, or being wrapped up tightly in layers of clothes or blankets.

Have a need for certain textures such as constant crunching or chewing on clothes, hands, hair or specific objects.

Sensitivity to temperature changes that may make the

child want to take clothes off, or put many layers of clothing on.

Being sensitive when wearing socks or boots, preferring to wear lightweight footwear with no socks (even in the coldest of temperatures).

Feeling restricted when wearing a hat, scarf or gloves. Many children find them to be itchy or uncomfortable.

It's important to recognise how your child responds to certain fabrics, labels, new clothes, etc. Then, if family or friends want to give new clothes as gifts, you can guide people on what to buy.

Hearing

Sensitivity to certain sounds, tones, pitch and level of noise, for example, alarms, bells, loud talking, traffic noise, musical instruments (drums, tambourine, etc.).

A child may become irritated by repetitive noises and music levels that are out of their control.

They may struggle to process people's voices in a busy crowded environment.

A child may experience one, two or multiple sensory difficulties. How they express their distress will typically differ from one child to the next. If your child struggles with sounds and specific noises, try a pair of ear defenders or noise-cancelling headphones. You can also try headphones with music to drown out particular noises. With younger children (or children with limited communication), you can try teaching them to put their hands on their ears if they are finding the noise is too sensitive for them to bear.

How to Create a Festive Sensory Setting for the Home

If your child responds well to sensory toys, it may be useful to put them a Christmas sensory box together. In it, you could put a snow globe, pine cones, different types of tree decorations (sparkly, textured, smooth), tinsel, candy canes, bells, a Santa hat, crunchy wrapping paper and baubles.

If your child enjoys making crafts, you could decorate a Christmas wreath together, using natural items such as fern, dried orange slices, dried berries, twine and leaves.

You could make a Christmas memory book, filled with all their favourite Christmas photos and then add to it every Christmas.

Maybe put together a container of Christmas toys such as squishy toys, books, jigsaw puzzles, games, colouring books, and so on.

If your child likes quiet chill-out spaces to desensitise, or they just like to be on their own, you could make a Christmas wonderland tent. It could be filled with a white (like snow) fluffy blanket, fairy lights, a mini tree, Christmas cushions, a Christmas stocking, books and

Christmas music.

You may already have a designated quiet room or space with lots of sensory items such as a fidget cube, lava or bubble lamps, fidget spinners, vibrating massage cushions, LED lights, etc. So, adapting to Christmas themed items shouldn't be too overwhelming for your child.

A quiet, comfortable space will be very helpful to your child when they need some time-out or quiet mini-breaks from the daily activities.

How you support your child throughout this overwhelming season will be entirely subjective to your own child's specific needs. As parents, we can only do our best when helping them and trying to understand their difficulties. The easier we make it for them to adapt, relax and enjoy Christmas, the better their experience will be.

How to Support Your Child when in New Public Settings

At Christmas time, you may visit new places such as public parks to see light displays, garden centres and shopping malls to go see Santa or to look at the Christmas decorations. Remember, when visiting new environments, your child is being removed from their personal comforts and familiarities. This can trigger anxieties and make their senses heightened.

Children and adults can really enjoy visiting and experiencing the Christmas décor, but with this, there can be additional stressors, especially if the place is crowded. Before visiting new places, maybe call ahead of time and ask if they have a quiet hour. Some places are now introducing an *autism hour*.

If you have a younger child and you are worried about them touching things, or wanting to pick things up, put measures in place prior to arriving. For example, use a set of child safety reins to prevent them from leaving your side. If they still use a pushchair, let them sit in it on these occasions, take a blanket or umbrella to help shield them from any over-stimulating environments.

For older children, maybe a wheelchair would reduce the stress and if they become over-stimulated, the child can sit calmly in the wheelchair as a place of safety.

If your child is at the stage where a pram or wheelchair wouldn't be appropriate, ensure you are aware of their toleration levels as you are walking around the new places. Are they getting triggered? Is it too busy, loud, and chaotic for them? Maybe build them up slowly, only go for ten minutes the first time then increase the duration the next time. They could take a home comfort such as a toy, a phone or an electronic device/tablet.

If an environment is too triggering for your child, for example, the music is too loud in restaurants or shops (which makes it impossible for your child to take part), ask the manager if they will make reasonable adjustments for your child, such as turning the music down or letting them go to the front of the cue.

As autism awareness is on the rise, businesses and employees are becoming increasingly accommodating and respectful of autistic people's needs. Remember, you can always ask members of staff for help. As employees, they are there to provide a service. Plus, adults are more caring when assisting a child and tend to be more inclined to co-operate when helping you.

How to Recognise when Your Child is Having Difficulties with Sensory Overload

When your child is experiencing a sensory overload, it can sometimes be difficult to differentiate between a child that is simply misbehaving or a child that is responding to environmental triggers.

A sensory reaction could provoke an autistic meltdown, stimming and unpredictable behaviours. The changes may present as the child being angry, uncooperative, irritated or annoyed, screeching, jumping around, spinning in circles, hand flapping, head banging, rocking, or withdrawal behaviours.

When in an overloaded state, a child's tolerance levels may be lower, which may cause them to become frustrated much quicker.

This is when you need to recognise what has triggered them and which sensory support or calming strategy needs to be put in place to help your child to desensitise and relax.

To help them, try to keep the environment as calm as possible. Don't talk 'at' your child frantically because it could trigger them more, and they may not have the ability to respond in their distressed state. Instead, try to talk calmly and quietly, try to help them by blocking out any additional triggers (lights, sounds, etc.), be their safety net.

Keep records of known triggers, so if your child is being looked after by another adult you can pass the information on maintaining consistency when your child is with other people. You can also track any changes, or recognise what reduces your child's triggers. As your child gets older, you may find they become less triggered and more tolerable when overstimulated, or they may worsen.

Personal Experiences

As a parent to an autistic son who has hearing sensory difficulties, I've had to be very mindful over the years when taking him to new places. When my son is experiencing change or anxiety, his noise tolerance is considerably lower. He'll react much quicker, becoming easily stressed and panicked.

My son used ear defenders for several years when outside the home, because he couldn't tolerate unpredictable noises. He also used them in the home when I was vacuuming, and so on. Over the years, he has learned to control and recognise what he can and can't process. He'll put his hands over his ears, or remove himself from the situation to prevent himself from becoming triggered. He is much more vocal about the feelings he experiences and how the noises impact him, this has helped us to work together and put in place coping strategies so he can manage his sensory difficulty himself.

I too have a hearing sensitivity. I would say mine is much worse than my son's. I take ear plugs in my handbag when out of the home, because I find most environments such as supermarkets, town centres and parks with lots of children running around to be unbearable. I can't watch the television at the same volume as my husband because I can't process the actor's voices when the volume is too high and the sound effects can be intolerable.

If I am in a busy crowded environment like the school playground or a restaurant, I struggle to converse with people because I can't separate the voice of the person that I am talking to, from the surrounding voices. I have to listen extra hard and most of the time will watch the persons lips so I can determine what they are saying.

Having a hearing sensitivity really impacts my day-to-day life. I have to be mindful of what triggers me because when I experience an overload, it can be excruciatingly painful which usually triggers me to go into an autistic meltdown.

Key Points

- Take time to recognise what your child's specific sensory difficulties and triggers are.
- Throughout the festive season, ensure all essential sensory support and coping strategies are prepared and put in place to help your child adapt and stay calm.
- Be mindful of your child's surrounding environment when in public places and new settings.

Chapter 3

Adjusting to Christmas Routines

If your family likes to put up a Christmas tree, share gifts and celebrate the festive season together, then your child will no doubt encounter lots of changes to their routines and familiarities.

The biggest changes that impact an autistic child are the ones that interrupt their day-to-day routines and living environment, such as:

Bringing a new Christmas tree into the house.

Decorating your living spaces with Christmas trimmings and decorations.

Making or bringing in new festive foods, e.g., mince pies, Christmas cake, gingerbread, Christmas dinner, and so on.

Changes in clothing, e.g., thicker, warmer (possibly Christmas themed) garments.

You may receive more visitors. The house becomes busier, louder, with increased socialising.

The house can feel more cluttered and overwhelming with all the additions.

You may be out of the house more, visiting family, attending Christmas parties or shopping.

As you might expect, each household will be different and like to celebrate Christmas in their own special ways. Therefore, the changes will be subjective to each individual child.

As a parent, you may already be attuned to your child's routines, recognising which changes can affect your child more than others. With that, your understanding of how to help your child to adapt to the changes should make the festive transitions easier to manage.

However, parents need to be aware that new difficulties can still arise for an autistic child. As they age, their specific needs generally change too.

How Does Change Impact Your Child?

If you are making changes to your usual décor, be mindful of how it can affect your child, for example:

Will you be making visual changes? For instance, will you need to move furniture around to fit in the Christmas tree, will it disorientate your child?

Will the tree have lots of lights on? If so, will your child love them or be visually triggered by them?

Does your child sensory seek via touch? If they have an impulse to touch everything, will your child want to pick up or play with the tree decorations?

If you put presents under the tree, will your child have the patience to not open them until you say they can? Does your child have anxiety associated with waiting? Will the long wait trigger additional behaviours?

Does your child become overwhelmed with cluttered spaces? Will all the new décor become unbearable as the days go on?

Will your child be triggered when all the Christmas decorations have been removed? Will you need to do it slowly, removing one item at a time?

Is your child prone to breaking things? Will the Christmas decorations create additional repercussions?

Can your child tolerate changes short term, but not long term?

Would your child prefer to have just one room decorated so they can escape the changes if need be, or would it not bother them?

If you are visiting family members and friends' houses

and you know they will have their Christmas decorations up, will you need to prepare your child by asking them to send you a photo of the changes (decorations) in their house so you can show your child before you arrive? This way, your child can transition easier to the new environment.

If the Christmas décor creates certain difficulties for your child then they will no doubt experience specific triggers and compulsions, which can impact their behaviour. Behaviour is a form of communication, so listen to and observe your child's reactions, this will help you to understand why your child is responding in that particular way.

Being Mindful of Unpredictable Changes

At Christmas, unavoidably, there will be many changes that are out of our control, such as:

> Changes in the shops, restaurants, and supermarkets, e.g., some shopping isles get moved around, they put Christmas décor in place, popular food chains introduce new food choices to their menus, etc.

> Television schedules change (showing Christmas movies and other Christmas associated programs).

> You may encounter lots of last-minute plans due to social demands from family members and friends.

There are many new toys, games, consoles, music, computers and so on, that are released around Christmas time to entice shoppers to spend their money.

Does your child have a special interest and will there be new additions released for their favourite activity? Will you buy it for them as a gift and if so, how will that impact them?

> Will they become over-excited?

> Experience changes in behaviour?

> Develop a highly focussed obsession with the new item?

> Become disinterested in joining in with the family, preferring to shut themselves off?

> Want to play with the same thing over and over again?

> Or will it not impact them at all?

Does your child have a particular bedtime routine with strict timings that they need to help them settle and sleep? If so, will there be changes due to additional social demands and activities? Will the changes impact your child if they don't get their required sleep?

Does your child have specific eating habits, meals times, and structured eating patterns of behaviour? If so, will there be any disruptions or changes?

Will your child become fixated on new routines, toys, food, decorations, etc.? Will it be difficult for them to adapt back to their normal routine?

Will your child need a break after Christmas to desensitise and relax?

During busy times, when things are changing from one day to the next, an autistic child may become highly dependable on their routines and structure much more than they usually would. This is because the predictability of routine keeps them calm and relaxed. With routine, there is no confusion about how the day (or week) may pan out. The structure prevents overwhelming feelings of being out of control of their environment and familiarities.

I'm not saying you can't make changes to routine, but rather to just be mindful of the dependency your child places on the routines and how the changes impact them.

Personal Experiences

Routines in our household are a must from the moment we wake up to when we go to bed. This is what works for us.

I have always had to be very regimented with my son because he struggles to retain certain information and has difficulty with instructions. I put a lot of visual aids on the walls around the house, such as posters with written instructions on how to do things and in what order.

For instance, our morning routine. He has an ordered list of how to do things such as, eat breakfast, clean teeth, get dressed, and so on. Having the sameness every morning keeps him motivated when getting ready for school. If I don't do this, my son becomes easily distracted, he would quite happily go and put the television on or just simply stay in bed. But, because he knows he has a set routine and has to do things by a certain time so he can get to school on time, this gives him solid focus in the morning.

My daughter who isn't autistic (she's eighteen months younger than her brother) is somewhat different from my son. She is very independent and likes to make her own routines. She will happily get herself out of bed, make her own breakfast, get dressed and so on. I never have to instruct her on what to do, or need to refocus her. They are both very different in how they function and process information.

My daughter will help to guide my son and help him to get dressed. He still struggles with buttons and putting his socks and shoes on. The whole process of getting dressed can be overwhelming and stressful for him at times. This awareness gives us the opportunity to help him and ease these difficulties he endures.

If we had no routine and if I was to leave him to his own devices, he would be a very anxious boy who suffered from meltdowns every morning, and no doubt turn up to school late and in a heightened state.

It's the same with Christmas. I have to keep his routine somewhat coherent with his usual day-to-day activities. We don't live close to family, so we tend to do a lot of travelling around Christmas time visiting people. I have to be mindful of my son's routines and try to keep them consistent when at family members' houses. I try to keep the meals the same and the same bedtime routines. My family are very accommodating and respectful of his needs.

When out of the home, I am hypervigilant of the environmental triggers around us, as I want the experience to be as enjoyable for him as possible. He loves spending time with family, even more so at Christmas.

Personally, I love routines. I like to plan, make lists and be organised, so this obviously bodes well for my son. If I don't, I can become very absent-minded and forget to do things, especially at Christmas when I know I have one hundred and one things to do.

On the downside though, I can become extremely fixated on my plans and routines and like them to run like clockwork. If my husband spontaneously changes things, it can completely throw me off balance and I find it difficult to adapt which causes me great distress. Having the awareness of how change impacts me really opens my eyes to how my son struggles too. Respecting each other's difficulties helps us to find a balance in our family.

Key Points

- Recognise if your child requires specific routines. Will their routine change at Christmas?
- How does your child cope with change? Do they need certain support to be put in place to help them to adapt?
- Can your child adapt to unpredictable changes in their routine? Will change impact their functioning and behaviour?

Chapter 4

Social Demands

Difficulties in communication and social interaction are core characteristics associated with autism spectrum disorders. Each autistic child will have different features and areas of abilities and limitations. This means that how your child interacts with people may be completely different to the way another child interacts. Therefore, each autistic child will need different forms of support.

Christmas time can be viewed as one of the most socially demanding times of the year. This is because Christmas revolves around people.

We become more sociable when:

Sending Christmas cards to each other.

Saying Christmas greetings to each other in passing, such as "Merry Christmas to you!" or "Hope you have a Happy Christmas and a Happy New Year!"

We might visit traditional Christmas plays and pantomimes.

Go to visit Santa and his elves at a specially assigned grotto.

Go for walks around the Christmas markets and displays.

Go to the shops for gifts, food and drink.

Join the family for dinner parties.

Give gifts to family and friends.

Get together for a family photo.

There are many factors that bring people together at Christmas. If your child has difficulties in communication, then it's inevitable that the social demands will in some way impact them.

Preparing Your Child for Guests in Your Home

When guests visit your home, will your child need preparations to be put in place?

What is your child's initial reaction and response when you tell them, *family or friends are coming over*?

Some children will love having people over and enjoy the interaction, but for others, it can be overwhelming and socially exhausting. If your child needs preparing, ask family and friends to not just turn up to your house without prior warning. If you let them know why and how the impromptu visits impact your child, then they may have a little more understanding of your child's needs.

You could say something like,

> "Could you please let me know what day you are coming and at what time? I need to let my child know when you plan to arrive, because he struggles with unpredictability and needs preparing for changes in the home. So, if you turn up unexpectedly, it can make him feel anxious."

When guests arrive, be mindful of how your child responds and interacts with them. Will your child interact straight away, or will it make them upset, anxious or shy? Does your child like hugs, a high five, a handshake, or no physical contact at all? This is another important factor that you need to inform your guests of.

Some examples,

> "When you arrive, my son may be distressed and shy, if you could just say 'hi' and don't overcrowd him. Just let him observe, then he will stay calm and relaxed."

> Or, "My child loves hugs, so if she keeps coming into your personal space and it makes you feel uncomfortable, just tell her politely, 'that's enough

hugs thank you.' She knows then to stop."

You may have a child that is overly sociable, or does not understand personal boundaries. In these instances, you may need to be mindful of how your child impacts your guests.

Does your child become hyper and excitable? Will your child overwhelm your guests, asking constants questions and talking 'at' them?

Does your child understand social rules and manners?

Will you need to explain to your child and inform them how to greet guests appropriately? For example,

> "When guests arrive, we welcome them in-to our home by saying 'hi, how are you?' Let them come in and sit down, don't overcrowd them too much."

Is your child sociable, but finds it difficult to make conversation? Give them some ideas of what to talk about, for example,

> "You can talk about your new game, they might not have heard of it or know what you mean, but it'll help you make conversation when talking about something that interests you."

If your child's differences in communication present problem areas for them, be mindful that it will take great effort for them to adjust to the typical *social norms*. Social skills require guidance and practice, just the same as when you learn any other new skill.

If your child is at an age where they are very self-aware of being autistic and their social differences, ask them if they have any specific social anxieties. Do they find certain aspects of communication to be difficult? For example, does your child recognise when it's their turn to talk, and to not butt in and talk over people? Does your child talk louder or talk *at* people instead of *to* them? Does your child recognise when they need to listen?

You could observe your child to understand their communication style and see if they converse differently with other people when compared to you and close family members (this can be recognised as *masking* their difficulties when around people).

You may get a clearer idea of what may be causing them to have difficulties if you can watch how they interact with a range of different people.

Your child may already be at a stage where they can express their difficulties to a guest. For example,

> "I'm autistic. I'm very shy and I struggle to talk in groups, especially when it's an odd number. I don't understand the dynamics of when it's my turn to talk. I prefer to talk one-to-one with a person."

Preparing Your Child to Visit or Stay at Other People's Houses

If you need to visit and stay with family and friends, be mindful that this can be socially demanding for your child. This may impact your child's attitude towards leaving their own home and their daily comforts. When at other people's houses, there will no doubt be changes to routine, environment, house rules, and so on. It will make it easier for both you and your child, if you can prepare your host with an idea of your child's needs, for example:

> "I limit the amount of sweets/candy containing E numbers and sugar because it makes him overly hyper, so I will bring our own snacks."

> "If my child is shy, it's not because they are being rude, they just need time to adjust to the surroundings."

> "If my child runs around in circles, rocks or flaps his hands, this is his way of calming himself. It's called stimming. He might do this when he is overwhelmed."

> "If my child becomes overbearing when playing board games, it's because she is particular about rules. She becomes overly fixated with winning, and can become distressed if she loses. We are working on this, and trying to help her enjoy the game, without it becoming too stressful."

Let your host know it is okay for them to ask questions. For example,

> "If you have any uncertainties regarding my child, don't be afraid to ask questions. Ask me about anything, I will try to answer it if I can. This way, it will make the visit easier for both you and my child."

You may have to explain certain things about your child that aren't viewed as typically age-appropriate. For example, an eight-year-old that is still in nappies (diapers) may be viewed as inappropriate for their typical developmental age. Explaining why a child has this difficulty may prevent the child from being viewed as lazy or slow and stop you from being judged as a parent.

The whole aspect of being in a different environment with other people may just become too much for your child to bear. It may trigger autistic meltdowns, withdrawal behaviours and anxieties. If this is the case, prepare your host for these changes in behaviour.

You may need to take your child into a different room, go for a quiet walk, sit in the car for ten minutes or listen to music. Whatever it may be, just recognise that you may need to remove your child from the situation so they can calm and de-stress. Your child may need time to adapt and process all the changes or the conversations. This can trigger a child to overthink matters and become overwhelmed with the complexities of the unfamiliar environment.

If your child finds it difficult to interact when in groups of people or when there are lots of people talking, it would be better to let them sit one-to-one with an adult or a child. This way, the social demand isn't as intense, allowing the child to interact without the added social stressors.

In some circumstances, you may find that it is best to leave your host's house earlier than planned. It would be advisable to prepare the host for the likelihood of unpredictable changes occurring, for example,

> "We may need to leave earlier than planned if my child becomes too overwhelmed with all the changes. We are working on supporting him in this area, to learn how to adapt and lower stress levels."

Then if you feel you need to leave it won't be such a shock to the host, or appear as though you are being rude and ungrateful.

Social Overload

If your Christmas involves lots of social activities, it is important to recognise that your child's tolerance levels when socialising will not be the same as yours.

Your child may become triggered easier and experience certain anxieties. Your child may need to depend on their comforts and coping strategies more than usual.

Try to recognise how other people can impact your child,

such as:

> Are there any irritating family members that trigger your child?

> Does your family like to celebrate with alcohol? Do they become unbearable after a drink or two, impacting your child?

> If there are lots of screaming children running around, can your child tolerate them? If so, for how long? Will your child become overly excited or experience social burnout?

> Does your family like to play loud music, sing, or play instruments? Does the noise trigger or overstimulate your child?

> Does your child get coerced into playing games or board games for which they just don't have the social skills, attention span or tolerance levels to maintain this level of interaction?

Another social aspect that has become very popular is to take photos or *selfies* on mobile phones. How does your child react to their photo being taken? Do they understand the concept of looking at the camera and smiling? Do they feel awkward if they have to cuddle in, touching the person next to them?

If so, it's important to respect your child's boundaries, and to inform your family or friends that they need to first ask your child if they are comfortable having their picture taken. Or ask them to show your child what you intend to do with them when taking the photo, so there are no unexpected surprises.

Recognise that at certain points you (or your child) may need to tell people,

"Time out, my child has had enough."

Communication is key when supporting your child. As a parent, it is important to recognise when you need to be your child's advocate and voice, working as a team to help them develop certain skills that will enable them to interact without difficulties.

Connect with your child, enter their world, see what makes them flourish.

There will be times when you know you need to put your child's needs before anyone else's. This is how you know you are responding appropriately to your child's differences.

Personal Experiences

I have many anxious memories of my son regarding socialising and communication.

From around the age of eighteen months and upwards, my son had difficulties with new faces. Other than my husband and me, he could only tolerate seeing my mum and my grandparents. For many years, anybody visiting the house would send him into a huge meltdown. It took almost a year of my in-laws visiting for him to become comfortable with them coming into our sitting room. Anybody else, he would just scream the house down. He was the same when he started nursery at two years old, any strangers entering the building would trigger him.

This unfamiliarity of faces and adapting to new people made it very difficult for us when leaving the house or going to new places. If people tried to engage with him, he would find it very upsetting. My son was language delayed; he was preverbal until the age of 5. The language barriers created a lot of confusion and uncertainty for him.

Now that my son is older and has gained full reciprocal speech, he can adapt to new faces just fine. He still has some anxiety surrounding certain social situations, for example, I have to prepare him for changes with new school teachers, and so on. The impact of the change isn't usually vocalised by him, the impact usually shows as an internalised anxiety, such as a tummy ache, headache, or disrupted sleep patterns. Thankfully, his teachers recognise this at school, so he gets a lot of support in this area.

My son will talk to new people, but it tends to be on his terms. He likes the conversation to be about his special interests, and he would talk for hours about Minecraft given the chance. But the social aspect of making general conversation doesn't come easy to him. He will need guidance and prompting, his attention will veer off, so I find I have to call his name to bring back his attention.

Recognising his communication ability and limitations has helped him to develop this aspect of socialising. He doesn't have any set friends; he tends to be a floater, but this is what he likes. I never force him into any social situations that I know he doesn't have the interpersonal skills for, I'd just be setting him up to fail and create further anxieties for him.

Key Points

- Recognise how your child uses communication and social skills when interacting with others.
- Have an awareness of your child's main areas of difficulty. What support do they need?
- Have the required social preparations been put in place?
- How do family and friends impact your child socially?
- What are your child's social limits?
- Does your child suffer from social burn out or need down time?

Chapter 5

How to Support Your Child in an Educational Setting

Christmas is not only celebrated in the home, it's also celebrated in a child's nursery, pre-school and school environment. Typically, today's generation of children spends a large part of their childhood in full-time education. Children become familiar with the routines, teachers/staff members, school children/friends, mealtimes, and their surrounding environment.

How your child celebrates Christmas in their educational setting will be determined by their age and what type of setting they are in.

The typical Christmas traditions we tend to see in an educational environment are:

Making Christmas decorations, singing festive songs, wearing Christmas-themed clothes, having a visit from Santa, making Christmas-themed cookies, having a school play, and so on.

With that, there are many changes, uncertainties and activities that can impact an autistic child.

Firstly, a child's routine may become disrupted. Educational settings are very structured and thoughtfully planned. This allows teachers to follow the syllabus, ensuring all children get the required education so they can meet specific targets and goals. This structure can be crucial for an autistic child when in this type of environment.

As mentioned in chapter three, autistic children can be somewhat dependent on routine for self-assurance and familiarity. It also helps them have a clear understanding of the day's activities. This reduces anxieties, allowing a child to comfortably transition from one task to the next. Changes in routine and additional new activities can become overwhelming for the child which can impact their well-being, reducing their willingness and motivation to take part in new tasks.

If your child needs preparing and additional support put in place regarding all the changes, it may be beneficial to ask the teacher if they have a plan of the activities (changes) prior to the festive season. Some educational settings may send out a calendar of events in advance to the parents, with information about the forthcoming activities.

It's important to recognise whether your child will benefit from prior knowledge of what the changes to routine are or if it will create additional anxieties. Each child will be different in how they respond, some may like the break from their regular class routine but for others, it may be problematic.

These changes can make them anxious and reluctant to go to nursery or school. The child may appear nervous and withdrawn, not wanting to join in. When arriving home from their educational setting, they may need longer to desensitise and relax. Some children experience tummy upset and headaches due to the constant stress and effort it takes for them to keep it together during the day. Meltdowns may become more frequent, sleep can become disrupted, triggered by feelings of anxiety and worrying. Fixations on special interests may become more intense than usual, and so on.

This is where the teachers and parents have to be mindful regarding the child's emotional and mental well-being. It is imperative that the child receives the required preparations and support when experiencing problematic difficulties.

Potential Problematic Christmas School Traditions

Christmas Cards

The long-standing tradition of sending Christmas cards is slowly declining because of improvements in technology such as text messages, social media, and so on. Children don't typically use technology as an adult might, so the tradition of sending Christmas cards to friends is still a favourable past-time activity that is carried out amongst the younger population.

You may have a child that has no interest in sending or receiving Christmas cards but if your child wants to take part, just remember that writing out lots of cards can be a task in itself. It's important to recognise:

> Does your child have the attention span and tolerance levels to sit and write lots of cards?

> Will they prefer to write a few at a time/will you need them to spread the task out over a few days?

> Will you need to write their cards for them?

Is your child a confident writer? Do they have dyslexia (difficulty with interpreting words, letters and symbols), or dyspraxia (difficulties with fine/gross motor movement, which can impact how a child holds/grips a pen)? If they do, this will inevitably influence their writing skills, and may require additional support.

There's also the issue of who to send the cards to. Will your child remember all the children's names? If they forget someone will it cause them to worry and stress over the unsent cards?

> How will your child respond to receiving cards?

> Will they fixate on who has sent them one and who hasn't?

Will they expect to receive a card in return for the ones they have sent?

Will your child feel upset if they don't receive as many cards as the other children?

It's common to hear of autistic children being left out due to their social differences. They may not have established as many friendships as a non-autistic child; therefore, this can impact the interaction they have with children.

As adults, we may think of card giving as just a simple task, but for autistic children, the social aspect of giving and receiving cards can create many unpredictable challenges.

Wearing Christmas Themed Clothes

Some educational settings like to have a Christmas jumper or a dress-up day. If they normally wear a standard uniform, the changes to clothing can impact autistic children significantly. This is because there are many sensory aspects involved with clothing. The changes in clothes can be too itchy or scratchy, too hot or restricted. There may be irritating tags or labels, or it may just be that they have difficulty adjusting to the concept of a non-uniform day. So being mindful of what your child can tolerate is important.

The differences in clothes may also impact them visually because of the unfamiliarity. Some autistic children may experience a cognitive face perception disorder called Prosopagnosia. This is also known as *face blindness.* This means a child may have difficulty with visually recognising and processing the people's faces when not in their typical uniform or clothing.

The visual changes in clothes (such as colours and themes) can be visually overwhelming, which can also impact how an autistic child recognises and interacts with people. For some autistic children, the changes will have a detrimental impact on them, and it's not uncommon to hear of parents keeping their child at home on these themed days.

I'm not suggesting you prevent your child from attending these themed days, but you may benefit from asking their teachers to be mindful of how they respond and react in these unpredictable situations.

Christmas Lunch

It is common for children on the autism spectrum to have many difficulties regarding food. Many will have their specific routines and food selections that they will only eat. This can be because of many factors such as sensory difficulties, food intolerances and sensitivities, digestive and bowel issues and so on.

If your child has particular difficulties with food and they are in an educational setting where they provide a Christmas lunch or party food, it's important to recognise if your child can adapt to the menu changes.

Due to health and safety policies, most educational settings are legally obliged to inform parents of specific menu changes. This allows the parents to inform the educational setting of any dietary needs their child may have.

If you think your child will have difficulty with the menu changes, it's important to recognise how you can prepare them so the change doesn't create any additional issues.

Another aspect which may impact the child is where the Christmas meal will take place. Will it be in the same location as previous meals, or will they move it? Will it be the same number of children or more or less?

If there are more children, will it be louder and more crowded than normal? Will it be in a compacted space and does your child become triggered easily in an enclosed environment? Can your child get out to a safe/quiet space if need be?

Your child may be able to tolerate the differences in food, but find the whole social aspect of the Christmas lunch to be too overwhelming. Many children (especially younger children) will sit under the table to help them calm and to feel safe. Some children will require ear defenders or ear plugs in these situations because the noise level can be torturous to the ears.

Visit from Santa

Will your child's educational setting receive a visit from *Santa*?

As discussed in chapter one, it is important to

acknowledge how your child will respond and react to a dressed-up character (Santa). If your child is ok with it, you may not need to prepare them, but for those that have issues it's important to find out if your child's setting does this activity, and if so, when are they doing it? This way, you can inform the teacher of your child's worries and put the necessary preparations in place.

If your child receives a gift, will they want to open it straight away (in their setting)? Some parents like their child to wait until Christmas morning to open all their gifts together, some parents don't mind when gifts get opened.

If you inform your child beforehand of what they are allowed to do, this can reduce the keenness of wanting to open it and reduce any associated stress that it brings.

Christmas Plays, Shows and Carol Services

Will your child take part in a play, show or carol service?

Christmas is the one time of year where parents get together to see their children put on a heart-warming performance and make you feel proud, but for some parents, it's not that simple.

Performing in front of lots of people can feel very daunting and scary for many children, but more so with autistic children that have difficulties with the social aspect of performing.

Standing up in front of a crowd can feel very intimidating,

especially when a child has difficulty with eye contact, talking in groups, being in crowds, and being the centre of attention.

This can cause feelings of anxiety because of the pressure of getting it right. If your child is a perfectionist and quite obsessive about doing things in a certain way, they may have an image in their mind of how they want things to play out. If this doesn't go to plan, it can impact their emotional and mental health because of the high importance they place on the task, viewing themselves as a failure if it does not meet their expectations.

A child may feel uncomfortable and awkward and, at times, feel out of control of their emotions. This can trigger them to enter a fight-or-flight response, which may shut them off, trigger an autistic meltdown, or cause an uncontrollable outburst of crying.

Many autistic children are emotionally and mentally delayed compared to their peers. So, it's important to recognise if your child may need more support in this area (especially in the younger years). If a child's mental and emotional health is impacted, it can have a ripple effect on other aspects of their emotional development, impacting confidence, self-esteem, and how they view themselves.

Personal Experiences

My son has always had exceptional support in pre-school and primary school. When he was in pre-school, he had limited language. He had words (cat, car, train, red, blue, etc.) but no reciprocal language, meaning he didn't converse or respond to language in the typical manner. I couldn't say to him:

> "What did you do today?" or "What did you have for lunch?"

because he didn't have the typical social skills to be able to understand and respond like a child of his age.

My son was also developmentally and emotionally delayed. He had very little understanding of his environment and what was happening around him. He spent the day mostly in his own little happy bubble.

I remember the first Christmas show he was in (at pre-school). The children had spent weeks practising the songs and actions. I arrived with my husband early so we could get a good seat. As we waited patiently for the show to start, all the children lined up in front of us ready to sing. My son, on the other hand, was totally oblivious to everything that was going on. He was distracted by all the new faces, and I could tell he was very unsettled.

As the children began to sing my son just ran around, going from side to side, in front of all the parents and children. I just wanted to hold him and stop people from staring at him. Luckily, a member of staff persuaded him to go over to her. He then saw me across the room so came running over to me and sat with me throughout the entire show. He was happy and comfortable, and that's what mattered to me.

I'm not going to lie, as I sat there, my heart sank. Not because my son wasn't performing, but because I felt like all the parents were staring at him and judging us. They didn't know about his autism and that he viewed and experienced the world completely different to their children. I would have loved for him to be able to stand up there, just like any other proud parent would. But comforting my child was more important than forcing him to do something that he clearly didn't have the interpersonal skills or language ability to partake in.

When my son started primary school, his language had developed to ten-word sentences, but he still had limited reciprocal language and still very much played in his own happy little bubble.

As the year went on, he developed socially and emotionally. He began to understand his environment better and this enabled him to join in with his first school play. It was the first time where he had joined in and understood the reasoning behind the task and what his teachers expected from him. He had a one-to-one support teacher that ensured he was okay.

As I stood there watching him, my emotions took over. I just wanted to cry with such an overwhelming feeling of pride. I couldn't believe my boy was joining in and was doing just fine. He was happy and fully aware of what was happening around him. It's a memory I'll treasure forever.

Key Points

- Will the Christmas changes in your child's educational setting impact them negatively?
- Will the Christmas activities cause/trigger anxiety or emotional stress?
- Be mindful of the additional social aspects that revolve around festive traditions in your child's setting.

Chapter 6

Challenges Associated with Christmas Presents

There are many things to love about Christmas - the decorations, Christmas food, parties and spending time with loved ones. For a child, one of the most exciting elements is receiving gifts.

Traditions centre around the story of Santa bringing presents down the chimney on Christmas Eve and placing them under the Christmas tree. This tradition leaves parents footing the bill and with the task of fulfilling this tradition.

There are parents that absolutely love everything about Christmas, from the cooking, cleaning, organising dinner parties, shopping, wrapping gifts, visiting the Christmas markets; they will happily cram as much as they can in over the festive season.

But for other parents, Christmas can also be very stressful and overwhelming, trying to juggle all the activities, balance finances, get the Christmas dinner ready, and not forgetting the added stress of shopping and buying gifts, wrapping them, hiding them, and just hoping that they've found the right toy.

Preparations for Gift Buying

In the current literature, autism spectrum disorders are categorised as a neurodevelopmental disorder. This means that autistic people have certain characteristics that develop differently to non-autistic people. We generally see development delays in young autistic children that are associated with communication and social skills, how a child interacts and reacts to their environment, and how a child connects with the world.

There will be many children that are mentally and emotionally delayed which may impact how they interpret presents, therefore, misunderstand or be oblivious to the whole concept of gift-giving.

If your child is developmentally delayed, you may find you have to encourage them to open the presents, and show them what to do.

For parents of typically developed children that haven't experienced this with a child, it can sound very odd. Why wouldn't a child want to open a gift? If a child has no understanding of the activity, then they may not realise that there is something inside the wrapping paper. Therefore, it may take them a little longer to connect with the activity.

A child may be disinterested, leaving the parents to open them. To get the child interested, you could let them open a toy that will excite them and engage them visually, for example, something with lights, or buttons that can be pressed to make noises and so on.

You may find they just want to play with the packaging or wrapping paper, the sensory aspect of touch may be more stimulating and enjoyable.

If your child is at a younger age or they have a sensory need to put things in their mouth, do they like to rip things up such as wrapping paper, or find little objects to put in their mouth? It's important to be mindful if a child has this sensory need, for example, cardboard books can be better than paper books as they don't rip so easy, or large Duplo bricks can be better than Lego sets if they like to put small objects in their mouth.

As a parent, you will no doubt already be aware of what your child can and can't have but it is also important to let other family members know too, so it won't be an issue when receiving gifts from them.

You may find your child has set ways of opening their gifts, for example:

The child is happy to open one toy, but then becomes disinterested in the rest. If that is what makes them happy, take the stress out of opening the gifts and let them open them when they are ready. This can also be an indication next time to only buy a few gifts, maybe focus on buying one toy that they really like.

A child may have difficulty moving from one gift to the next. You may need to use a 'now and next board' to show them how to move on to the next activity. It may be that the child is happy with the toy, becoming fixated, and doesn't feel the need to play with anything else. If it takes for instance, three days to open gifts, then let them enjoy it that way. Try not to place typical expectations on your child.

A child may want to organise the gifts, or open them in size, colour or shape order, for example, open all the round ones first. This may be visually stimulating for them.

If the room is busy and loud with lots of people, this may be overwhelming and a trigger for your child. It may impact their tolerance levels of sitting for a period of time focussing on the activity of opening presents. Again, this is where parents need to be mindful - can your child sit through ten minutes of opening gifts with others? Would it be easier to let your child open theirs separately, earlier or later in the day?

A child may want to feel, shake or squeeze every gift. This sensory characteristic may help them feel calm or it could be their way of expressing excitement.

A child may become overwhelmed with lots of new things all at once. If so, keep it simple by buying gifts that they can relate to and like. If your child has a favourite drink or snack, like chocolates, Pringles or gummies, etc., wrap one of those up. I've seen parents buying crates of diet Coca-Cola for a child as their main present. The child was overjoyed and would have been happy with just that.

A child may become confused about what the toy is. You may need to set time aside to show and explain what it is and how it works.

A child may not like toys at all. This can make buying presents very difficult. For example, a child may be interested in just playing computer games and already have their favourite game. Trying to buy things or introduce new ones may be a waste of time because they have such a limited interest.

Opening Gifts

If you have a child that has no difficulties when opening gifts, and can happily rip off the paper speeding through them like a whirlwind, then this section may not apply to you.

However, many children have issues with hand dexterity (fine motor skills). This impacts coordination and finger movements, therefore influences a child's ability to open gifts.

Sellotape and sticky-back tape can be difficult for them to open. The grabbing and ripping off the paper can also be problematic. If a child has difficulties, you could:

Leave one edge of the wrapping open, allowing them to just put their hand in and pull the item out.

Use gift bags.

Cover a box or a shoe box in Christmas paper, put the toy inside and let them just lift the lid up.

Use a Santa sack.

If you need to use gift bags or boxes, explain the situation and why this is important to family members who are buying gifts for your child. Ask them to use these also, or provide them with the appropriate packaging. Or, you could tell them you will wrap them or re-wrap them to reduce anxiety for your child to a minimum.

Save any salvageable Christmas bags, boxes, etc., for next year (if you have storage space). Ask family members to save any unwanted gift bags/packaging for you. Then next Christmas, you can just bag it, box it and done. Saves time and saves your child from getting stressed.

Other Useful Tips

Buy lots of batteries/rechargeable batteries (if you're buying battery powered toys).

Pre-charge all chargeable powered items.

Take off any annoying plastic (where possible) to make it easier for your child to open their gift.

If your child is impatient, and likes to play with things straight away, pre-build items like a ride on toy, a bike, doll's house, etc. You won't then waste half of Christmas day building things (unless you don't mind of course). This will also help alleviate stress and anxiety for your child.

Read the instructions or download them prior to giving an item to your child which you know they will need help with. If you already have a clear understanding of how to work the new item, it may make it less stressful when you come to show them how to use it.

Look how to turn things on. Obvious, I know, but technology these days isn't always that simple.

Use the same wrapping paper (colour/theme), or place easy to recognise stickers on gifts so that your child can easily recognise their presents.

If your child has anxiety surrounding surprises, use clear cellophane style wrapping, so your child can see through the packaging, and they still have the enjoyment of opening something without the associated anxieties.

Have a bin/trash bag ready to collect the wrapping paper, or have a designated area to put all the rubbish. Give your child a container of some sort or a specific area to place all of their gifts to reduce the chaotic environment and mess.

Another way to reduce stress is to be organised. Again, it may sound very obvious, but it's surprising how fast popular toys can sell out around Christmas time. If you know your child collects or likes specific things, picking presents up early will take the pressure off of you.

Luckily, we now have many options when it comes to shopping which allows us to reduce the stress of trying to find specific things, such as online stores, and websites. Amazon, eBay, Facebook marketplace, local selling sites, etc., are very popular for picking up cheap inexpensive toys.

A child can also look online or in catalogues to get a visual idea of what they want, to help prevent any unexpected surprises.

It is common for parents to ask (older) children what gifts they would like, and to write a *wish list*.

This can be helpful for both you and your child, but remember, your child may not understand your 'rules' of a wish list.

If it's you that pays for the gifts, then it'll be you who decides what they can and can't have, and whether you let them pick their gifts or not. Will you say all the gifts are from Santa (if they still believe in Santa) or say the big gift (main gift) is from of you?

Their expectations may not be achievable. To make it easier, explain what they can or can't have, for example:

> 'It's a list of wishes, it doesn't mean you will get each and every gift that you write down.'

Give them a limit of how many toys they are allowed to pick, or a specific value if they understand money.

If they want something popular, or an item you know may not be available, be realistic and tell them they may not be able to have it. Have a back-up plan, ask what they would like instead if you cannot get the preferred gift.

If your child asks for something that isn't your typical norm (you may think it's a silly choice), like a fifteen-year-old boy/girl wanting to collect Peppa Pig toys (which are aimed at pre-school children), respect their preferences. If you are happy to buy them, will they be pedantic and need to pick the toys themselves?

Social Aspects of Giving & Receiving

There are many challenging social aspects, when receiving gifts, for example:

A child may not know how to respond in front of people. They may feel excited and overjoyed inside, but feel awkward or find it difficult to express their feelings.

When other family members are cheering happily, saying,

"Look what I got, isn't this amazing!"

many autistic children will have no interest in sharing the

joy, or know how to reciprocate the joy for someone else's possessions. They can appear disinterested or rude for not sharing the same excitement.

A child may have limited social skills which may impact how they use manners when receiving gifts. They may snatch, without saying thank you or showing any appreciation because of their specific communication style.

A child may be engrossed in the opening of gifts and just simply forget to use manners.

You may need to show or explain to the child, how and why you would like them to say thank you and how to be respectful of other people.

A child may be completely the opposite and be very particular about manners and how people appreciate their gifts, getting upset when people don't show gratitude towards others.

Children that find interaction difficult, may become easily triggered, their anxiety may be heightened which can result in an abrupt short temper. They may respond differently to normal in their heightened states, making their behaviour appear to be of a spoilt brat and ungrateful. They may erupt into boisterous unpredictable behaviour and lose control.

A child may become overly excited, wanting to open everything quickly, not knowing who bought it or where it came from (e.g. from relatives). This can be difficult when wanting to thank the person who bought the gift. Perhaps, keep those gifts separate so you can see who bought them, or make a list of who bought what as your child opens each one.

As long as we are mindful of a child's expectations and specific limitations, we can make the experience enjoyable.

Personal Experiences

Due to my son's developmental delays, gift-giving in our house wasn't typically what you would expect with a young child.

My son had difficulty with his fine motor skills, so for his toddler and pre-school years his dad and I opened most of his presents for him. It wasn't until he was around the age of five almost six, that he really grasped the concept of presents. My son has always had narrow interests so rarely gets excited about receiving gifts.

If I was to ask him,

> "What would you like from Santa this year?"

he couldn't grasp the fact that this guy he had never met would bring him presents. Because of this, we said,

> "Mum and dad will buy you the main present that you would like, and Santa will bring you a few other gifts."

This way, on Christmas morning it saved the confusion of this Santa guy popping by, instead, he could relate to the fact that his dad and I had put presents under the tree for him.

My son would always ask for gifts that I couldn't get. One year, he was highly focussed on a particular brand of Japanese toy cars, that you could only buy overseas. It would have cost a fortune in shipping, and the toys weren't cheap, so I had to ask my son to choose something else. He then asked for a toy that was only sold in the USA. Once again, the shipping and customs charges were much higher than what the actual toy would have cost. I had to explain, I could only get him something from the UK. At his age, this is inevitably difficult for him to understand.

He then asked me for something that really took me by surprise, he said,

> "I want a baby, not a toy baby, a real baby. That I can hold and cuddle."

He loved babies (and still does). When we go out of the house, and he sees a baby in a pram he will get all excited and want to go talk to the baby. Well, no surprise, that was another gift that I couldn't get him, unless I magically produced a baby in three months' time for Christmas Day. A baby most definitely wasn't in my plans!

Key Points

- Be mindful of how you wrap the gifts, and put any required preparations in place (charging electronic devices, read instructions, and so on).
- Recognise if your child can withstand the time needed to open gifts with family members, for example, will they become bored, stressed, triggered, overly excited, etc.?
- Be prepared for behaviour changes, e.g. the child being over/under-stimulated.
- Don't expect your child to respond to gifts in the typical manner. Let go of all expectations and make your 'own rules'.
- Be aware of social differences, for example, that they may not express feelings of joy, misunderstands social rules surrounding manners, etc.
- Bear in mind that autism interests may be somewhat different to conventional hobbies and fascinations.

Chapter 7

Choosing the Perfect Gift

Buying gifts for children can be an exciting time. Knowing you'll see their happy little faces on Christmas morning, making lots of special memories is what Christmas is all about. But getting the gift just right can be complicated.

If you have a child that has certain interests, and knows exactly what they want, then that makes buying gifts for your child much easier. However, for those that have limited areas of interest, it can make present buying very stressful.

There are many things to consider, such as:

A toy that may be age-appropriate, may not necessarily be developmentally appropriate.

Does your child get bored easily? Do they play with things only a handful of times and then never again?

Does your child like surprises? (YouTube has made surprise toys very popular, for example, blind bags, surprise eggs, LOL Surprise dolls, and so on).

Or, does your child hate surprises? Would they prefer specific things, finding it difficult to adapt to new toys? Do they need familiarity to feel comfortable?

With younger children, if you are buying pretend play toys, such as a kitchen with plastic food, or a doll and pram, do they understand the concept of pretend play, or see it as literal, e.g. 'that's not real food, why would I pretend to eat that?'

Is your child a sensory seeker? Would they enjoy toys that are stimulating? For example, if they love strong smells, would they like a bottle of perfume or aftershave? Or a basket of bath bombs or scented bubble bath?

Would your child appreciate things for their bedroom decorated with their favourite themes/characters, making it a place for them to relax and visually pleasing?

Does your child love to learn new facts or like to read imaginary stories? Many children love fantasy comics or non-fiction books focussing on science, animals, flags of the world, and so on.

Does your child have a talent relating to music? Would they love to learn how to play a musical instrument?

Buying gifts, especially for children that have literal thinking or specific ideas and expectations regarding what they would like can be stressful for the parent, but the child can also find it just as challenging. For example:

"That wasn't on my list! I don't want that!"

A child may have a set idea of what they expected to receive, taking the idea of a wish list too literal. Also, a child may find it difficult to control what family members buy them, becoming pedantic about what they want and don't want, finding the whole situation difficult to comprehend.

Likewise, a child may find it difficult to understand that everybody has different interests, expecting everyone to like what they like, therefore, thinking everyone should receive gifts exactly to their liking.

Somebody may buy a child something that they personally love and feel the child will love it too. If a child is set in their ways, they can appear disinterested and rude when new things are introduced.

If a child wants to buy gifts for family members or friends, they may buy them items specific to their liking and not what they think the person would like, for example, if the child loves unicorns, they buy a unicorn teddy for their mum, a unicorn cup for their dad, a unicorn t-shirt for their sister, a unicorn pen for their grandma, and so on.

If you have an older child and they want to buy you a gift, be mindful of the situation. Do you need to be literal to prevent them from becoming stressed about what to buy, or can they happily pick you something?

It's common to hear autistic people saying,

> "I have no idea what to buy you. What do you need or want?"

Help them out by guiding them. Does your child need you to be direct, or do you need to give them a hint of what you would like? Would they be ok with choices? For example,

> "I like the HUGO BOSS Red perfume, and I also like pink, silver or gold heart-themed Pandora charms."

First, I have been direct, giving a specific perfume that they know if they buy it for me, they won't get it wrong. Second, I've let them pick a charm, but given guidance on exactly what colour and style to buy. This gives them a visual and a clear inclination taking the stress out of having to find an appropriate gift.

Or, if your child wants to buy you a gift of their choice, just remember, they are buying you what 'they' think you will like, not necessarily what you want, but they have tried. If, for instance, they buy you a pink headband with black spots on because they love it and would like to see it on you, remember to wear it. It's the thought that counts.

Which brings me to children's thoughts and vocalising their opinions. If your child is literal in their speech and has no filter, will they respond with comments such as,

Mum to child: "Do you like my new jumper that grandma got for me?"

Child: "No, it's awful!"

Mum to child: "Have you enjoyed your Christmas Day?"

Child: "No, I didn't like the food, I don't like that I had to sit with the family all day when I could have been playing my computer games, and don't like that I had to join in."

This could just be bad-mannered behaviour, or it could be because the day didn't fit their expectations of what they thought Christmas Day would be like. Having changes in food, routines, and being socially interactive all day may not be their idea of an enjoyable day.

Being Mindful of Your Child's Gift Expectations

If you buy your child a new item of clothing, will they expect/require a particular fabric, colour or style?

If you buy them something different to their typical norm, will you need to explain why you have changed or purchased that gift? For example,

> "Your favourite toy was getting old and tatty, so I wanted to get you a new one. I couldn't get the exact

same item, but this one is similar."

If your child receives a favourite toy, will they expect to receive more of the same/similar toy? For example, a child may love buses, and expect everything to be associated with buses because that's what they love.

Be mindful of their interests, don't just buy them what 'you' think they'll like. Take note of their comforts and what excites them.

Behaviour Changes

Some children can become stressed with a gift that they don't like. This can cause feelings of guilt because they find it hard to get rid of something that someone has thoughtfully bought them. A lot of autistic children become attached to toys/objects. So instead of parting with it, they feel guilty for feeling like they are stuck with it. This can stress them out or come across as a tendency to hoard.

Be mindful of your child's sensory triggers, for example, if a family member receives perfume and they spray it, can your child tolerate the smell?

If your child is overwhelmed and experiences an autistic meltdown, will you need to remove them to let them desensitise and calm down? Can they quickly integrate back into the triggering environment or will adjustments need to be made?

What to Buy?

If you have a clear idea of what to buy your child, you may not need the following information, but you might get a few additional ideas.

First of all, I can't say exactly what your child will like because I have never met them, so obviously I won't know what would be age-appropriate for them, but what I can do is suggest frequently associated toys for autistic children.

Sensory Toys:

Fluffy or fleece blankets, weighted blankets.

Disco lights, a lava lamp, fibre optic lamp, LED lights.

Tambourine, bells, rainmaker/shaker, etc.

Rubik's cube.

Fidget spinner, fidget cube/snake, stress balls.

Trampoline (brilliant for circulation, burning off excess energy, destress, etc.).

Swing set, ball/sand pit, slide.

Music streaming device, Bluetooth speaker/device for playing music, Bluetooth or cable earbuds/headphones.

Developmental/Interactive Toys:

Puzzles, jigsaw puzzles, board games.

Melissa and Doug educational toys.

Duplo bricks, Lego sets, Mega Bloks, Meccano sets, K'nex sets, model building kits (Airfix).

Knitting/sewing/tapestry kits, art supplies, Play-Doh, clay/modelling supplies, Aqua beads sets, jewellery making.

Electronic tablets, computers, hand held consoles (can utilise development apps or games).

Books, colouring/puzzle books, comics, magazines.

Musical instruments.

Dinosaurs, farm/zoo animals.

Science kits.

Popular Themed Toys:

Thomas the Tank Engine, Peppa Pig, Harry Potter, Power Rangers, WWE (Wrestling figures), Action Man/Barbie, Star Wars figures, Marvel/DC figures, Baby Annabell, My Little Pony, Fisher-Price Little People, Vtech Toot Toot playsets.

Vehicles – Matchbox cars, Hot Wheels, JCB construction

vehicles.

Disney – Movies, character toys, clothes, games.

Computer games (check age restrictions) – Minecraft, FIFA football game, Fortnite, Roblox, Hello Neighbour.

Blind bags/eggs – Lego Mini figures, L.O.L Surprise dolls, Shopkins, Num Noms, Trolls, Thomas and Friends Minis, Hatchimals, Tsum Tsum, Mash'ems, Playmobil, Sylvanian Families.

Imaginary Play:

Camera, kitchen/shop/till and money, ride on car/bike, toy hoover/sweeping brush, doll/pram and accessories, toy musical instruments, dress-up costumes, doll's house.

Personal Experiences

For my son's first Christmas (he had just turned one years old), we didn't buy him too many toys because of him being so young and not needing much. We noticed that he loved to rock back and forth (little did we know, this was a form of stimming for him). So, we bought him a rocking horse style toy (it was actually a caterpillar). He loved it. My son didn't want to play with anything else, he would just spend hours and hours sitting on it, rocking back and forth. If he wasn't on his caterpillar, he would sit on the settee and throw his body back into it, back and forth really hard. He also had phases of head-banging on the floor and walls. At the time, we knew this wasn't typical behaviour and this was when we started to notice his differences.

The following year, we bought him a battery-powered Thomas the Tank Engine train set. He still had no speech at this point, so I spent a lot of time watching his body language so I could respond to his needs. He liked the train track to be set up in a circle, and would always want two trains to be running on the track. He would get down on the floor with his head turned to the side so his ear would be pressed against the carpet, with his eyes fixated on the trains. He'd have his bum up in the air as he pushed himself around the outside of the track on his knees, following the train round and round. If the trains caught up with each other and derailed, he would have to start all over again. This would go on for hours at a time.

Around the age of three, he started to copy me saying, "Choo, choo!" Even though he had no language or conversation, this breakthrough of repeating these sounds was just amazing. He was very happy watching his trains go round and round and I was absolutely overjoyed that it helped him to use his voice.

We continued buying him Thomas toys, mainly the Take-n-Play die cast toy trains. About a year later, he could name every single train (around thirty of them). He would line them all up in a row, and with his finger, he would walk along touching each one saying their name, it was unbelievable. He couldn't tell me he needed a drink or say his sister's name, or any other typical language skill, but he could say every train name and remembered them all.

After this, we worked on numbers, he would count everything, even when we left the house, he would count everything he could see. We then developed more words through books. I bought lots of picture books and got library books with themes, for example, in the home, at the park, at the zoo, etc. I would name all the items in the pictures, such as a bed, door, window, swing, slide, and so on. Over the years, he picked up lots of additional words, and by the time he started school he could use very basic language. To me, that meant everything, because I knew he would begin to copy and repeat now that he was slowly understanding context.

My son is now eight and has full speech. He still has difficulty pronouncing certain words and finds it tricky when pronouncing his R's, W's and sometimes V's and F's. He has done amazing; I am so proud of him, and it all began with Thomas the Tank Engine.

I can't bring myself to get rid of that train set, or his Take-n-Play trains, I will cherish them forever, they bring very happy memories.

This Christmas, my son wants his own PC (personal computer). He loves the Minecraft and Planet Coaster games. He has recently been on a computer coding course for 7-10-year-olds because he loves to learn, so I know a computer will be very beneficial to him. He's not particularly interested in toys anymore, not like he used to be. He now just likes Lego City sets, or Lego mini figure blind bags. So, as you can imagine, his Christmas morning is very predictable. He will always tell me which Lego sets he wants, and I tend to add a few Lego-themed gifts, like books, t-shirts, stickers, etc.

Key Points

- Be mindful of your child's expectations and thought process.
- Does your child love or hate surprises?
- Do you need to buy toys specific to your child's special interests?
- Will the toy choice trigger behavioural changes?

Chapter 8

Christmas Planning and Preparations

First, it's important to remember that what works well for one family may not necessarily work well for another. There is no one size fits all Christmas plan.

How you plan and prepare your Christmas celebrations for your child, will be determined by many factors, such as:

Is your child developmentally delayed?

Can your child effectively communicate?

How old is your child?

What is your child's understanding of Christmas traditions?

Family influences:

> Do you partake in some or most of the Christmas traditions?

> Are you married/in a relationship or single? Do you spend Christmas with both families?

> How many children do you have? Do you have more than one autistic child (do they have different interests/needs)?

> Will you be doing lots of travelling over Christmas?

> Will you have financial stresses?

And much, much more.

With that in mind, I will try to give a selection of ideas that can be useful. Some may be suitable, some might not. You can pick out the points which you may find beneficial to your situation.

Preparations

Create a calendar, chart, diary of events, or whatever it is that suits you and your child so you can have a clear idea of what is happening over the festive period. On it, you could put things like:

> The day you are putting the tree up with decorations. You could put a picture or sticker of a

Christmas tree on the specified day, as a visual aid.

Family events/gatherings. You could put photos of the family members with names, etc.

Places you will visit, such as Christmas markets, pantomime, Santa's Grotto, and so on. You could show them these places on the internet (business website, YouTube, Google Maps, etc.) or print off guides/details for them to look at.

Mark days when you know you will have visitors. Again, you could place photos of the visitors.

If you have work commitments that will impact your child's routine (parties, working later than usual), try to put those days down. If there will be last-minute changes, decide if it's best to write those plans down nearer the time, or can your child adapt to the changes?

Write down or put pictures of any Christmas activities/traditions you intend to organise for the home, for example, watching Christmas movies (you could put a picture of popcorn, the movie, etc.), making a gingerbread house, making cookies for Santa (Christmas Eve) and so on.

Helpful Lists

Lists can be very helpful to keep you organised, especially when you are busy and have lots of activities happening around you. Lists such as:

> A checklist (for your child) when leaving the house or going to visit relatives. On this, you could put phone/electronic device and charger, noise-cancelling headphones, sensory kit, a favourite toy, snacks, and so on.

> A house-cleaning list, so you can keep up to date with daily chores, or let others see what needs to be done and to tick it off when they have helped you.

> A food shopping list. If you know your child needs specific foods, ensure they will be in stock, or if you can, buy them ahead of time so you have them ready for when you need them. Christmas seems to be the one time of year where everyone stocks up and fills their fridge and cupboards, it's common to see supermarket shelves bare throughout the festive season.

> Make a gift buying list for your relatives, so you can keep track of who you need to buy for and whose needs wrapping, posting/mailing, etc.

Sensory Plans

If your child requires sensory support, some ideas for planning ahead could be:

Make up a generic sensory kit or box for your child. You could put this in the sitting room, or if you are travelling put it in your handbag/backpack, car, etc. You could put things in it like:

> Ear defenders, ear plugs, sunglasses/coloured lenses, fidget/sensory toys, colouring pens and paper, a book/puzzle book, mini travel game, a favourite drink/snack, blanket, comfort toy, headphones and a music device, an electronic device/tablet.

Be mindful of your child's diet over the festive period. Autistic children that have genetic predispositions, tend to have difficulty with digestive issues, inability to detox toxins effectively, skin conditions, ear, nose and throat issues and many more. In these circumstances, food will inevitably impact how the brain and body responds and reacts. Pay attention to:

> Processed foods, sugar and E-numbers. These can act as stimulants. Synthetic chemicals, additives and preservatives which can be found in many of these types of foods, can impact the adrenal glands (causing them to over produce adrenaline, cortisol, etc.), and stimulates the nervous system.

This can influence sensory triggers, for example:

> Heighten anxiety, can make a child overly hyperactive, disrupt sleep patterns (because the body cannot relax because of the excess stimulants/adrenaline in the body), cause mood swings, make the child feel jittery and irritated, cause the skin to feel itchy due to excess

inflammation in the body, and so on.

If you already know of any sensory or mood triggering foods, monitoring what they eat will help your child immensely. This will reduce the chemical (imbalance) and hormonal reactions, helping them to be less heightened. This then enables the child to be calmer, allowing them to have better control of their sensory and environmental triggers.

Involving Your Child in the Preparations

One way of making Christmas enjoyable for your child could be to involve them in the decorating of the tree. If you are particular about how you like the trimmings, and this is something you prefer to do yourself, perhaps let your child feel involved by having their own specific decorations, or buy them their own tree ornament to place on the tree. Let them just touch that one, but none of the others. Or let them have a mini tree of their own to decorate for their bedroom, or put lights or tinsel in their room.

Let them choose some of the Christmas activities. It may be something as simple as drawing Christmas themed pictures with them, or dancing around the room to Christmas music together. Do they enjoy making puzzles or playing board games? Maybe let them pick a game for Christmas Day? Either way, allowing your child to have some input will inspire them to join in.

If your child still puts food and a drink out for Santa on Christmas Eve, pick and prepare them together. You could even make it silly and fun by putting out your child's favourite snacks. For instance, my son loves *Kinder surprise eggs* and the fruity drink *Vimto*, let them share their favourite things with Santa.

If you decide to incorporate the Elf on the Shelf, you could have a breakfast welcome/farewell party together. Make it fun by having a novelty theme, such as red and green napkins and straws, and foods that they wouldn't usually have for breakfast, something they will find fun and enjoyable.

Being Mindful of Your Child's Needs

Ensure all parents, siblings and family members are familiar with the plan (events, days out, etc.). This way, you can all communicate and work together to help things run smoothly.

If your child has a developmental delay, differences in communication, or struggles to process certain information, check with your child to see if they have understood the changes that will impact them directly (for example, Christmas jumper day). If they need to be shown social stories, or visual cues (like YouTube videos, drawn/written guides, etc.) try to help them, this will lessen their stress or misunderstandings.

Give your child time to process the changes. If your child can communicate, ask them if they understand. Have them repeat back to you what you have discussed, so you know they aren't going to have any anxieties with change and so on.

Would it be beneficial to do a practice Christmas day, or a 'meal trial' (if possible, in November or a week or two before the main event)? If so, you could make up a dinner of the main items that your family will be eating. See if your child needs any of the foods adapting or changing. You could take a photo of the Christmas dinner meal and put it on your visual planner, so on the day of the event your child will know what to expect.

If you start your Christmas celebrations on the first of December, will your child find it too difficult to wait twenty-four days until they can open their gifts? Do they struggle with anticipation or heightened anxieties, which may cause stress or behaviour changes?

Will they hold all the tension inside, let it build up, then when Christmas Day comes, erupt? Would it be better to have one day just for opening presents (left to play with no distractions), then the next day do the Christmas dinner and celebrations?

Will one month of changes be too much for your child to tolerate? If so, would it be better to only have the changes over a two-week period or less? Some parents like everything to go back to normal as soon as Christmas Day is over and done with. If there are parents that feel like this, a child may experience those feelings too.

Anxiety tends to be an intrinsic element of being autistic. I'm not saying all autistic children experience anxiety, but it is very common. For that reason, it's important to recognise this characteristic, and to be aware of possible triggers.

When it comes to the present wish list, remember to be mindful of their interpretation of a wish list.

If your child needs to wear a Christmas themed jumper/outfit for nursery or school, buy this ahead of time and familiarise your child with it by letting them wear it and see if they are comfortable. If not, you know to change it, or to let their class teacher know if your child has difficulties with this tradition.

If you are visiting family or friends and you know they will be providing a meal, remember to contact them prior to the event to ask what the food choices are, just in case you need to make adjustments to your child's meal.

Personal Experiences

I love Christmas and I love to be organised. I tend to buy gifts for my children throughout the year. Not only because I like to be prepared, but because it spreads the costs, and most importantly, it means I don't have to spend December shopping or looking on the internet for gifts. I can spend the Christmas season doing Christmas activities.

I also shop earlier because I hate wrapping gifts. I find it is very time consuming and I don't have the patience or attention span to sit and wrap for long periods of time. So, I like to take a picture of what I have bought (so I don't forget), then wrap them as I go.

I like to get the Christmas tree and decorations out in the last week of November (ready for the 1st December). I like my son to see what we have and show him what I intend to put up around the house. We look at the tree decorations and talk about which ones are his, and about our memories of buying them.

He's always picked dachshund (sausage dog) themed ornaments. We had two dachshunds, a girl and a boy. We still have our 13-year-old boy, but sadly lost our girl eighteen months ago, we miss her lots. So, no doubt this Christmas, when we get the tree ornaments out, we will have lovely special moments remembering her together (which already brings a tear to my eye and a lump in my throat). I just love that my son expresses this sentiment.

December generally runs smoothly for us. We like to

spend the Christmas festivities with family, so I like to have December planned out in advance.

Both mine and my husbands' families are all spread out, so don't live close together. My son really doesn't do well with travelling. One of our journeys is a five-hour drive. From the moment we set off, his anxiety will start. He will want to know where we are going, what we are doing, who will be there, how long we are staying for, and so on. His anxiety will get worse and worse as the journey goes on. Every two minutes he will ask,

> "How long 'til we get there?"

He will need frequent reassurance because the stress of travelling and going somewhere other than his home brings on enormous erratic thoughts. As soon as we arrive, he'll be reserved for a while, but then eases into the celebrations and relaxes just fine. After a day or so, he will nag to go back home, because the changes become uncomfortable for him and too disruptive to his routines. As soon as we leave, the anxiety starts again and he will dissect the journey. When we arrive home, he gets emotional, because he's so happy to be back in his comfort zone with his familiarities. He'll say,

> "I really missed the house and my bedroom. I don't want to go away ever again."

Even though he enjoys visiting and staying with the family, the whole process of it all is too much for him to tolerate. My non-autistic daughter is the opposite, she will cry because she wants to stay with family and doesn't want to go home.

This is where planning for us becomes essential when supporting my son's needs. When travelling we let him visually see the Sat Nav, so he can watch the time scale, where we are going and how long is left. We set up movies on a travel DVD player for him to watch, to try to divert his focus away from travelling and give him fidget toys to keep him stimulated if need be. My son loves Lego, so he likes to have a Lego vehicle with lots of wheels that he can spin and take apart and put back together.

My son becomes clingier when around other people. When he's out of his comfort zone, he likes to link arms with me and snuggles his face into my side when people talk to him, becoming very shy. I try to prepare him with social scripts so he can respond in these types of situations. I also try to guide his conversations with others, prompting him with things I know he understands and can relate to. Otherwise, I don't think he would interact or learn how to use his social skills effectively.

Key Points

- When making your Christmas plans and preparations, remember, there is no one-size-fits all method. Do what you need to do to for you and your child. If it means stepping out of the traditional norms and making up your own rules, then don't hold back in doing so.

- Have a clear plan for your family's festive activities. If you need a visual calendar or lists to keep things running smoothly, ensure you put the preparations in place.
- If possible, involve your child in the preparation process, but remember to be mindful of their needs.

Chapter 9

Christmas Aftermath

When the festive season comes to a close take time to recognise how you are feeling, because it's very important to look after yourself. We spend weeks running around after everyone else ensuring Christmas goes to plan that we forget to ask ourselves,

"How am I holding up, do I need a break?"

Don't feel guilty for taking a moment to see what you need.

I'm sure most parents of autistic children will agree that parenting a child with additional needs brings many challenging moments and feelings of despair and that's before the added inconveniences of Christmas.

The festive season can be filled with long unpredictable tiring days. Christmas not only disrupts your child's routines, but yours too because Christmas is not your child's typical norm. It may not necessarily be because they don't enjoy Christmas, but because it brings many uncertainties and unexpected moments of unease.

You may have had days when you felt like a failure, there may have been moments when you struggled to enjoy the festivities and wished it was all over because you felt you couldn't meet your child's needs. Just remember, there is only so much you can understand or do for your child, you are doing your best.

You may have had some days when all you wanted was for your child to just relax and enjoy the magic of Christmas when in reality, all Christmas brought was additional meltdowns, anxiety and stress.

You may have found all the family gatherings to have been too socially demanding for you and your child, thinking that next year, instead of planning Christmas around other people, you're going to have a quiet, peaceful time all on your own away from extended family. Don't feel guilty for putting your child's needs first.

When stress is heightened, you may find you are less tolerant of your child, which can impact how you are as a parent. Just remember, try not to place any expectations on having a picture-perfect Christmas, take each day one step at a time.

Be mindful of yourself physically and mentally and how Christmas impacts you. Your child may be oblivious to the additional stress of Christmas, therefore, not understand why you may be tired or struggling. There may be external stressors, for example:

> Feelings at this time of the year may be extra sensitive if you have loved ones that are no longer here.

> Financial burdens can cause a strain on a marriage/relationship.

> A house that is more cluttered and messier than usual can become irritating and triggering.

> Additional cooking and cleaning can be challenging and tiring.

> Shopping can become a burden; car parks are busier, cues are longer, people's patience is tested, things may be sold out, and so on.

> You may have had a tougher time with your child having additional meltdowns or unruly behaviour, which can become mentally and emotionally draining.

Being mindful of your own needs and finding what reduces your stress is just as important as looking after your child's needs. Take time for yourself, whether that is sitting quietly listening to music, having a soak in the bath, reading a good book or going for a quiet walk. What-ever it is, remember to be kind to yourself.

Time to Reflect

When you get a moment, take time to reflect on what went well and what didn't. Take mental notes, or write things down so you can look at them later in the year and be somewhat prepared for next Christmas, such as:

What specifically triggered your child?

Were there any particular foods they liked/disliked?

Were the Christmas decorations triggering? Were there any decorations they particularly liked?

Were there any toys and gifts that were a waste of time or money?

Were there any nursery/school activities that induced stress?

Were there any activities that your child particularly liked that you would like to do again next year?

Which preparations worked well and you know they would be beneficial for next year?

Were there any traditions that confused your child? Will you need to explain the truth about Santa next year?

Did any particular shop or visiting a person's home

become triggering for your child? If so, what were the triggers?

Did you use alternative wrapping techniques? If so, did they help your child?

Were family members accommodating of your child's needs, or were they stress inducing?

How did Christmas impact your child's mental health and well-being?

Did any changes to routine impact your child?

Which is easier, having people come to your house or going to theirs to celebrate? Or does it not create issues?

Did you have to make new traditions or have to adapt any current ones?

Did grandparents or any family members have any issues or place unrealistic expectations on your child?

Did you experience any specific triggers?

If you are in a large family that places a big importance on being together to celebrate the festive season, take note of how this impacted you and your child. Did it all go to plan, or were their many changes and adaptations that need to be put in place so you could effectively support your child?

Did you feel pressured when going visit family worrying about how your child would interact or behave amongst others? Or did you have feelings of guilt if you didn't visit, feeling like you let them down?

Or do you have a smaller family, or a family that has a quieter Christmas with not so many social demands? Did this allow you to meet your child's needs, could you keep to routines and familiarities?

Did you have a chilled Christmas, preferring to just go with the flow? Does this method work better for you?

Either way, each and every family will plan and celebrate Christmas in their own unique way. You do what's best for you and your family.

Lastly, whether you and your family have a fun-packed or chaotic Christmas, each and every child will experience their own unique autistic Christmas.

I hope you enjoy every moment, filled with lots of joy and happiness.

Take this special time to create autism bonds and remember,

Every child is a gift.... xxx

Thanks for reading!

Amazon reviews are extremely helpful for authors.

Please add a review on Amazon and let me know what you thought. Thank you.

Emma xxx

Also available from Emma Kendall

Perfectly Autistic
Post Diagnostic Support for Parents of ASD Children

This helpful book covers areas, including:
ASD Terminology.
Helping your child understand their ASD diagnosis.
Helping your child how to explain to others they are diagnosed with an ASD.
Teaching your child how to advocate their needs.
Calming and coping strategies.
Autistic Behaviours.
Emotional connections and self-confidence.
And much, much more.

Order direct from www.amazon.co.uk

Printed in Great
Britain
by Amazon